Love Poems
from Me to You

I will love you forever

Love Poems
from Me to You

I will love you forever

TERRI ANN DANIELS

ARPress
ILLUMINATING IDEAS
EMPOWERING VOICES

ARPress
45 Dan Road Suite 5
Canton MA 02021

Hotline: 1(888) 821-0229
Fax: 1(508) 545-7580

Ordering Information:

Quantity sales. Special discounts are available on quantity purchases by corporations, associations, and others. For details, contact the publisher at the address above.

Printed in the United States of America.

ISBN-13:   Paperback   979-8-89356-552-2
              eBook   979-8-89356-554-6
              Hardback   979-8-89356-553-9

Library of Congress Control Number: 2024902571

Table of Contents

Oneness

It takes time to truly love
Someone,
To get beyond each other's
Facade.
So often, we try to tailor
Ourselves to be who we think
We ought to be for this person
Or that.
I'm glad you and I have taken
The time to make ourselves
Totally clear, as transparent
As we can be.
Slowly, we've explored our
Oneness, learning the needs
We each to each fulfill
And there's no doubt in my mind, I love you.

The Way You Hold Me

It's nice to be held, hugged and gently
Kissed.
I'm not fragile, but you touch me as if
I need tender care and I can tell that's
The nature of you.
At night our bed feels like an oasis
In the dark, a private retreat from
The cares and conflicts outside.
Every morning
I love seeing your
Face and feeling you next to me.
I'm glad we have each other.
My life would be empty
Without you and your tender care.

If I Was a Painter

If I was a painter like Dorian Gray,
I would paint your portrait and hang
It in the attic alongside mine.
We would have years and years
To be together.
Everyone would marvel at how young
We looked, but only you and I would
Know the secret and our love would
Go on forever.

TERRI ANN DANIELS

Walking in the Rain

Yesterday we took a walk in the rain.
We walked down to the ice cream parlor
Around the corner.
Both of us fit nicely under a huge umbrella
I found in a thrift shop last fall.
As we walked along, with our arms around
Each other, I made you laugh with one
Of my sillier jokes.
I want to think your laughter means
You're still in love, still mine.
When we started I didn't expect forever
From you. I didn't think that forever
Was what you were looking for.
Now, I just live and love you one day
At a time, one more special day
I'm lucky enough to have you love me.

A Day at the Beach

Yesterday, we walked on the beach.
We held hands and picked up seashells
And twisted driftwood.
We went down to the pier, then along
The shore and up to the rocks that were
Getting splashed by the ocean waves.
It was one more page in our book
Of memories we're slowly creating.
Your touch, that slight off-kilter smile
Are becoming imprinted on my mind.
We share so many of the same opinions;
Conclusions we've come to alone,
Before we met.
I'm not someone who agrees just to make
You happy.
I have to be my real self even if that includes
A bit of clumsiness.
Sometimes, I wonder where the tide of events
Will take us.
Where will we be and what will we be doing
This time next year?
I hope I'll be with you walking along the beach,
If only in my mind.

Looking Back

Looking back, I contemplate the times
I have retreated and closed myself off
as much as I could from the intrusions
Of the world.
I still, meander and stay behind my own
Private door, thinking about
The vagaries of my life, the decisions
That have brought me to this point.
Always, I've left a peephole to see who's
Knocking, but you're the only one
Who has a key.

Finally

I remember the day I finally
beat you playing chess.
You were clearly disconcerted, but
I could tell you were trying not to show it.
Not that you're an egotist at all, but
I guess my victory came unexpected.
When you said you couldn't play again
For two or three weeks, I accepted
Your reasons without any skeptical looks.
Mentioning it in the faculty newspaper
Might have been a little much, but then
All is fair in love and ego.

TERRI ANN DANIELS

Yesterday

I would really like to revisit yesterday
And all the other days we've spent together.
I remember one school days very clearly
Kissing you in the Chem. Lab closet after
We both volunteered to get the supplies.
I realized the teacher knew.
He had a slight smile on his face
When he pulled me aside and suggested
I should leave the gathering of the supplies
To others.
He had a wistful air that day.
I imagine he was probably remembering
His own supply gathering days.
I guess everyone has them in one way
Or another.
We all wish we could visit yesterday.

Sitting in the Rain

Now that we're back together
I'm going to try to be more
Understanding, to listen better
And really hear what you have to say.
Being apart from your smile made me
Realize just how much I need you.
It was like sitting in the rain, waiting
For the sun to come back.
I realize now, you are the essence
Of all that is good in my life.

Faded Photographs

At times, when we're holding each other
And I'm looking into your eyes,
I think of all the years to come
And all the love I have to give to you.
I hope, deep within me, when those years
Have turned to faded photographs,
There will still be long moments of you,
Holding me, looking into my eyes.

Alone

Being alone and lonely is
Not something you get used to.
Its something you deal with
While waiting for the next smile
To come along.
Like everyone else, I've been
Trying to find the right person
Who has been trying to find me.
Finally, accidently, we met.
Since then, you've been constantly
On my mind.
Each time we talk, I like you more.
It's almost impossible for me to
Hang up the phone when you're on
The other end.
And, when we're actually together,
I am Totally immersed in this private club We have created.

Hero

My friend Barry is depressed.
He's just been written out of the third
Seson of Law and Justice.
Have to leave.
All of his friends deeply sympathized.
It was the type of role actors people
And pray for.
He hated to tell his wife that he was
No longer a sergeant in the law and
Justice universe.
He could tell she thought of him as kind
Of a hero, even thought it was all
Make - Believe.
Everyone like to be the hero, sometimes,
Even if its just for the changing a tire or
Chasing the bad guy on Tuesday evenings
For an hour.

Maybe This Time?

Have you ever hoped that someone
You were desperately attracted to
Would somehow, in some way begin
To be romantically interested
In you, too?
You hope that the romance that wasn't
There on Monday would miraculously
Appear on Tuesday.
You begin to interpret everything they say
or do in terms of love or not love.
No matter how handsome or beautiful
The would-be lover is, everyone falls
For the unattainable at one time or another.
For some, it might be the first instance
Their desire was denied.
They say, "The heart wants what the heart
Wants," but sometimes the heart can't get
what it wants,
Not now, not ever. But maybe this time?
Maybe you?

TERRI ANN DANIELS

To a Long - Time Love

I wanted to say, love me
But, we had just met and you
Can't do that then.
So, we danced and laughed
and looked for tomorrow in each
Other's eyes.
And, waited and wondered just
How would it end.
Would the phone ring?
Would I go?
You called and we went,
And soon we were two.
Us against the world.
Years later, I still love you.

To You from My True Self

Everyone has a facade they show to the world.

Behind the facade is their real self.

The self that stays hidden most of the time.

Most people know exactly who their real self

Is, but most have no intention of letting anyone else know.

Still, I think that everyone has at least one person who knows what

they're really like.

It's probably a wife or husband or their last friend

From high school.

There's always somebody.

For me, it's you.

I try not to use any artifice between us.

I always try to speak my mind, maybe

Sometimes, too bluntly, but always truthfully.

You are the one person I totally trust,

The one person that actually knows all

The light and dark sides of me.

Thanks for being there and letting me be me.

TERRI ANN DANIELS

Independent People

We're both independent, self-sufficient people.
We read and study books that often have
No interest for the other. And, our taste
In music is eclectic and very different.

Your idea of good sport is a long hike
While my idea of an exciting sport is anything
that involves a ball.
Yet, we've found in each other someone

To share a special togetherness and I'm glad.
I don't want to drown you in me or depend
On you for decisions I alone should make.

Instead, I need just what you are:
A caring partner who neither leads
Nor follows, but walks beside me with love.

Come to Me with Laughter

I've been wondering how we manage
To laugh all day long.
I've tried to analyze it, but I'm afraid
Of losing the magic by too much
Judgement.
Sometimes, I feel like such a clown.
You always laugh at all my jokes, even
The one-liners that are only mildly
Funny to me.
Of course we always leave time
For tenderness and a few moments
Of lively poignant thoughts.
Not to mention our excitement
In the moonlight darkness.
It seems we've had a good recipe
For being content all the time
You're like a happy pill to me.
One dose and I'm set for another 20 years.

TERRI ANN DANIELS

I Have Kissed you

I have kissed you everywhere I can
Kiss you.
In the movies, in the living room, outside
In the garden, inside the laundry room,
In the car, on the streetcar, in the shadows
Beside the apple tree, in the pool, on a hike,
Even on the tennis court.
I will kiss you everywhere I can.
I think of each kiss as a gift.
I am rich with your kisses.

Just for Awhile

Just for awhile,
I wish you could be me
And see yourself with my eyes,
Think of my thoughts and feel
The excitement I feel when we're
Together, touching, kissing, stroking,
Then you would know how much
I truly want you.
Each time we do make love
Is incredible.
The pleasure you provoke
Explodes within me
Again and again ang I lose myself entirely
In the sensual sensations of you.

TERRI ANN DANIELS

The Sound of Your Voice

I love to hear the sound of your voice.
Sometimes, when I'm alone I play
Your words back like a recording
In my mind, enjoying our conversations
Like I enjoy your touch.
Your voice feels like a caress,
Sometimes soft and sometimes
Roughly gentle.
I'm beginning to know the hidden
Essence of you.
I've come to undersand, the need
To accept each other as we really are,
And, learing this,
I choose you to love.

Just Because

Because we're together
Everything in my world seems better.
Colors are brighter,
Flowers smell sweeter
Even my work flows smoother
Day to day
At night as I sink into sleep
I can feel your love covering me
Like a blanket of tenderness.
When I awaken next to you
I feel reassured.
I know, then that I'll have one more day
Of happiness,
One more day our lives will rhyme.

The Waterfall

Always
You excite me.
I like to pretend the shower is a waterfall
And stand under it kissing you,
Feeling the soap, slippery,
Between us
as we hug and laugh.
Oh yes,
Always you excite me.

Hugging

I just want to know,
Hugging you is something
I really love to do.
To feel your body against me,
Pulling me into your cozy warmth
Filling all the cold and empty
Spaces within me.
As you nuzzle my neck
You make me delirious
With your scent and your touch.
Yes, hugging you is something
I really like to do.

Older

I guess I feel old because I am older.
Looking in the mirror I can see there's'
Grey in my hair and lines at the corners
Of my eyes
I don't know how the got there.
It's as though they crept in one day
And became a part of me before I knew it.
I really don't mind.
Perhaps my friends will think I've acquired
A new maturity.
In my eyes, you look the same as ever.
It seems we've grown old together
And I don't know hoe it happened.
Looking at you, I can believe in forever
And I feel grateful you are still
My whole world.
My existence needs the touch of your hand's
And the smile you give me every day.
Your presence is all I need to know of love

Ride the Wild Copter

There are certain things you should do
Just because they are fun and unique.
One of these is to ride in a helicopter
and land on the roof of a tall building.
After we hesitated for days, watching
The advertisements on television,
we decided to go for a ride
in a helicopter ourselves.
We decided that you only live once and it
Was an experience we didn't want to miss.
The pilot swooped up and down, between,
And over the buildings, all the time narrating
A travel monologue that enlightened us
About the various sites we were seeing.
The ride was exciting and. nerve wracking.
I was afraid of falling and afraid of flying
Too close to the buildings.
When we were back on the ground,
We felt exhilarated.
We went home and jumped into bed
With our blood racing.
It was exciting there, too.

TERRI ANN DANIELS

In the Dark

Touch- seeing in the dark,
I have learned all of the secret
Places of you and I revel in
The knowledge and privilege.
Still, each new time we merge
Into one seems better than the last.
The pleasure you provoke excites
Me beyond reason and I know
we were meant to be.

Listening to the Silence

I like to sit in the dark
listening to the silence, contemplating
whatever is occurring in my life
and what has already happened.
The silence is never absolute.
It's always full of creaks and groans
and purrs and whispers.
It's these small sounds that make it
Seem alive.
They give the silence depth you can
Feel if you're careful not to stir.
Sometimes, my mind fills with old videos,
Each one showing a different scenario from
The past, lit with the memories that are still
meaningful to me.
The first time we held hands
walking home from school, that first kiss in the library, the prom.
I can still see you clearly even though it was a long time ago.
We were so young then and our older selves hadn't left
The shadows yet. They were just waiting in the wings
For us to step off the stage. After all, Life and the future do go on,
no matter what, no matter who.

Loving

When you read these poems again,

Maybe, just browsing from one to the other,

I hope you are thinking about me.

Wherever I am when you're reading,

I'll probably be contemplating you

And the last time we held each other.

 You've brought a lot of feelings to me

To sort out.

I can't say I always understand your moods

And whims, and there are times when

We clash.

But, my spirit needs you like my body needs

Food and water.

You've given me trust and good fortune and some

trepidation all at once.

Most of all, you're all I want of love.

www.ingramcontent.com/pod-product-compliance
Lightning Source LLC
Chambersburg PA
CBHW051251120626
46547CB00014B/1903